Michael Pedersen is a prize-winning Scottish poet and author. He's published two acclaimed collections of poetry, his second *Oyster* being a collaboration with Scott Hutchison. His prose debut, *Boy Friends*, was published by Faber & Faber in 2022 to rave reviews in the UK and North America and was a Sunday Times Critics Choice. Pedersen also won a Robert Louis Stevenson Fellowship and the John Mather's Trust Rising Star of Literature Award. Pedersen's work has attracted praise from the likes of Stephen Fry, Kae Tempest, Irvine Welsh, Maggie Smith, Sara Pascoe, and many more. Co-founder of the literary collective Neu! Reekie!, he is the 2023-2025 Writer in Residence at The University of Edinburgh.

Praise for *The Cat Prince*

'A brilliant book that guards its innocence with open arms'
Zaffar Kunial

'Searingly specific, exquisite and requisite.
I relished reading every tiny morsel of it'
Shirley Manson

'In this latest stunning collection, [Pedersen] touches on themes
of life-altering friendship, loss, nature and love'
Scots Magazine

'Every page of *The Cat Prince* brought me gladsome joy.
Pedersen has the astonishing power of finding the astonishing
in every moment that deserves a raised glass. This celebration
of life is partly achieved through his humorous way with
words that constantly made me laugh out!'
Daljit Nagra

'Endlessly boyishly playful, defiantly
un-macho and un-afraid to be daft'
Liz Lochhead

'If the alphabet is a piano keyboard then Michael Pedersen
plays it with the confidence and panache of a jazz improviser
who knows that every note can have the potential to change
someone's life. Be amazed by this book'
Ian McMillan

T0349812

THE
CAT
PRINCE
&
OTHER
POEMS

MICHAEL
PEDERSEN

corsair poetry

CORSAIR

First published in the United Kingdom in 2023 by Corsair
This paperback edition published in 2024

3 5 7 9 10 8 6 4

A CIP catalogue record for this book
is available from the British Library.

ISBN: 978-1-4721-5687-7

Printed and bound in Great Britain by
Clays Ltd, Elcograf S.p.A.

Papers used by Corsair are from well-managed forests
and other responsible sources.

Corsair
An imprint of
Little, Brown Book Group
Carmelite House
50 Victoria Embankment
London EC4Y 0DZ

An Hachette UK Company
www.hachette.co.uk

www.littlebrown.co.uk

for my
whiskered
& un-
whiskered
friends

We are all travelers in the wilderness of this world, and the best we can find in our travels is an honest friend.

> —Robert Louis Stevenson

To me it is as if a bit of myself had died, the romantic part, which was forever running after him.

> —J.M. Barrie on the death of his friend
> Robert Louis Stevenson

Contents

THE
CAT
PRINCE
&
OTHER
POEMS

Lines on the Melodies in Men

It is funny, I say to K, who's wading shirtless
in the burn, *the things we remember about growing*.
As a boy I played a game with my uncle
where I blew into his boxer's thumb
as he ballooned his muckle bicep,
the shoogly inkwork of his tattoos
smearing to a blur,
arms bulging bigger
with each puff I stuck him with
—stuffed solid as a cloud
before emptying its storm.

I blast another lungful down the thumb's
portal, slurp up the tobacco scum,
lick my lips like liquorice.
If they don't give it you, my uncle gruffs,
showboating his trophy muscles,
take it with these: a forced ending,
the cloven-hoofed *ars poetica*
of Danish Harri—Da's toughest brother.

Popeye arms, I faked coveting them,
knowing fine well
not even with a marching band
would I let that music in. It was
the physical play I loved, the luminous
swell, like a kissing ritual
without the kiss.

The melodies in men are sometimes
my arch nemesis, a neighbour's
tusk, the wicked nimbus
of a better version gunning
for my soft & silly. Though mostly

1

they're hot courage: brave bones stookied
in mucky fun, the buttress of friends
hatching bawdy superstanzas.

Together we might lay to rest our unclings'
bedraggled sermons, their *just
a generational thing, a not-in-our-blood
thing; an I-do-love-you-you-know-that-
but-fur-fucks-sake-I-shouldnt-have-to-
broadcast-it thing.* Just—oh. All
the possibilities of a river.

In the future, I tell K, *we will hear
each other better*—a friend
will clasp my hand and beg me be
in touch more often, to touch more often.
He'll say he's been thinking of me,
that he knows it's going to hurt
hellfire, all the while holding firm
as moon grips. Promise cast
not as we splinter into the next stage
but heartbeat-wet in the *herenow*. Words
as close to their import
as a sparked match.

2

boys holding hands

become men
holding hands
because learning
to dance starts
haptic & here
a rumple
of pinkies
the trill
of palms
another skin
blossoms beyond
its sleeve
another
fist unpeels
to fingers as bud
unhooks its petals
the anthesis
of the hand
for we are
best friends
slow sun's
gauche promise
hold me
as language
drifts
through the throat
of the wrist

Mike's Tackle Shop: The Ultimate Fishing Experience

I don't want to bash a trout in with a mallet
but I do eat them, so have done.
Contrarily, I relished my boyhood
fishing trips: the symphonic purr
of loch lap & naked talk.

This lament's, instead, for feeding the beast
—the machismo rigmarole
of school lunchtimes eked out
in Mike's Tackle Shop
sculpting a huntsman's facade
that might see a twelve-year-old
gatekeeper open the lock
on a jaunt away. To earn the invite
took fidelity: trawling shelves
& a feigned affection for the aggrandised
tales of young burnouts—gory
clobberings, spittle-riddled.

Beyond their gloat/this rite of passage
lay a lullaby of arcadian elegance—
where rods bow down
for plates of glass
as sun-shafts shred
to infinite flecks. Bog fairies & air
bubbling from another realm.

Ensnared by ritual, whilst ardent
as the light-lusty moth,
I found enough to heat me.
From the shopfront signage of *Shakespeare
since 1897* to the protest pong
of the doomed ragworm.

Of the flies, I spied their joyous plumage,
flamboyant haircuts, flourish
of glitter, tail & tassel, some
like fireworks, exotic birds like
tapestries, with such names:
the Golden Monarch, Wullie Gun,
Fallen Star, Lang Syne.

When the future revealed itself
in the hook-punctured face of a dead
pike—its punk lip & glam pout,
mad eyes both fire & coal—
I quarrelled myself invisible
& squeaked: why is everybody
hiding from the softness?

28/05/21—*that'll be that*

When Scotty texted to say his old man had died,
there was an undertone of sorry to bother you
with this hackneyed yarn, gelded & done to death.
Undertow aside, I was glad he was talking.

When Scotty texted to say his old man had died,
he mentioned he'd sat with him, notebook to hand.
I took this to mean: he wrote the light out of his eyes,
shackled by stillness until breeching the din.

When Scotty texted to say his old man had died,
it was just three lines long. Two half-sentences
connected by ellipses... one: a concourse
of blackheads... the other: the end of the line.

When Scotty texted to say his old man had died,
shrift & settled, the final point addressed all other
business. Though furnished with kisses—
wet beyond their x & ripe for the taking—it ended

in flowers.

What Grief Feels Like to Me

The first spot of unstoppable rot
on the leaf work, realising then
the roots have already been taken.

Feeding my old loaf of a heart
to the pigeons, baying for wing-break
amongst the scrum.

Bells, bells for eyes, ringing ragged,
not stopping until a tongue falls off
or the jar breaks. Either way, it's over.

Biting into mango & finding only stone.
The teeth, defeated, as if hit by rifle butt
—shot of metal & comes the blood.

A fish scaled alive, fine-tuned to every rip
of the madcap knife; stream's plash
agonisingly nearby.

A bird gone gonzo, trapped within a twist
of ribs, beating itself bloody
against the cage unbreakable.

In the beginning there was an apple
ready to be eaten: the dawn of taste,
followed by a death that begins all dying.

Like conjuring your best ever line,
then knowing it's lost, returning
to the margin to never do better.

The Cat Prince

I am the Cat Prince, I declare,
already on all fours, already balls-naked
in the house of Hastie, where there's Adam
(Hastie), Daniel & me—the Cat Prince.

We're boyhood budbursts, twelve years
of silly in us. Adam laughs frantic
gasps, guffaws, then pegs it
to his bedroom anticipating the chase.

Daniel, wavering between cat & laddie,
compañero & fugitive, succumbs
to the gnostic glamour—strips
for a full feline transformation.

Down to our little furs, little bloods,
ready to breenge past the chide
of absent classmates, who might well
hear of this and smite us with shame.

We are cuddle-kings hankering
for Adam's adulation—all moggy moxie
we embrace the cat life, vow
inurement to the side effects:

carpet burns, wind-lashed pimpling;
the sacrifice of language in each
falsetto yowl. As hunters we're tasked
by the Creator: our gaze

a crosshair; our pounce a ripple
of bravura. Who else so guilefully stalks
sunbeams? We'd do well here
—*it's those damn cats again,*

the neighbours would learn to yawp,
as I raced by with a robin redbreast
between my jaws & Daniel finished shitting
in their rhubarb patch. It's convenient

not to think of the killer in us,
holding back our purr, assassin-still.
As we coil our new cat bodies to a spring,
Adam clambers feart atop his bed.

What happens next is louder
than we hoped for. Adam's mum, startled
by the cacophony, arrives then screams,
curtailing the playdate. Later that night

she calls my mum, concerned,
though my mum never mentions this.
I can only assume she was wise to it
—the mythos, the hieroglyphs—fathomed

we'd soon meet the type of trouble
that could really shake boys down:
long days when the teeth tear it out of us
& the claws don't stop coming.

But not yet, I hear her whisper,
not without this moment's orchestra
of feeling. As a boy I was whiskerless,
weighed down by the nest of knots

squat in my belly. As a cat,
I was so much more. Of course,
as mother to the Cat Prince,
she knew all this.

9

Unfirmly Thatched

Quality thatching, this
fleshy huddle—our bodies grasping—
skin & petal: a rustic roof. Hope
bundled into yelms, stapled
with resolution by sways
of hazel sticks. Over hard winter's spleen
its balding, a spar coating:
fresh wrapping for festering wounds.

Yet one squall, one waver, can strip us
to the fragile rigging. The wretched shift
from OK to KO. Our little thatched heart
unravelled into dead stalk, water reed,
sedge, unpurpled heather.

Beware the blizzard, the stormy bits,
where trusted friends, in moments
weakened, lust after what we love,
possessed by the very same rapture.
Skewed: easy to hold the hammer, hard
to hammer home the blame.

Of the stodge in our bellies: a slip
on a drink too many, a thought
gone sloppy for the thrill
of being someone's newest ride.
Knickerless, risking everything
despite being unwilling to gamble
even buttons on it.

A thousand times it doesn't budge
until one day it does.
No melody to what happens here:
fire fed on junk

blazing through our treasured chattels;
possessions tossed on in panic
to plump up the smoking plumes.
To the haunting shadow, the hush
before the plunge: I'm sorry, really
really sorry. Please take it back,
before it's ash, goo, gone.

So maybe it doesn't, fright steadies
something yet to wobble and new day
arrives like fresh bread. Closer
for nearly being so far apart.

Och, our fecund cores, these scanty
laureates of love. Here we are
snogging, sticky, equally
terrified, all in on each other.
Praying the stitches
hold, the roof doesn't shred,
the scorch that kept the chimney busy
—our toes purring warm by the fire—
isn't throttled by wind. We
should never have left the tenements.
We should dry and stack the straw.

The Rain in Cushendall,

pot-plump, runs as if fleeing a trap. Racket-mongering
in language stone-auld; cheek-chiseling—
someone once kissed it with their eyes,
went blind. Stout pearls
prang onto each protruding tongue
daft enough to taste it, skin-bearers left reeling:
tongue cannae bruise—cin it?

Full metal jacket rain, porridging the soil,
              missiling into Cottage Wood's darkest fissure.
              Rain to rattle the rhododendron
              out its floral hubris, slake the thirst
              of every tentacle, gush on the sycamore's
              buried knots. An Irish hare,
      with two dead legs, limps beyond its shooting range.

A direct hit will wreck a chip, six
will flood an open supper; pothole to a puddle in ten
savage seconds. Yet never
has it blasted fierce enough to stop Kearney's Fleshers
slicing rashers or Johnny Joe's filling pints, so as
—warm-bellied, squelch-socked—local seers
might moot the weight in it:
whether it warbles, carries grit,
whether the graves are listening.

(A poem with a hat tipped to 'The Rain in Portugal' by Billy Collins)

let the lilac in

having hared through the day
let me be your armchair
by the night window—unhaul,
coorie in; into this cradle
of salt & buffer inject
those wayfarer bones; douse down
the day's flare of voices—
see the restless gritters sleep
or, better still, delete themselves;
be held, a pebble lagooned
in water's midnight minerals;
behold moon plated in the eyes
of an owl—starlight's lapidary scrawl
rallying the dark like hot ash caught
on spiderweb; the luminescence
graffiti-ing your slippers
& sloshed onto the chin's timber;
hush now, as, on my lap, you begin
a dreamer's mumble,
somnambulant lips kiss the air
until finding my skin

Queensferry's Lost Not Found

—for Scott

It's something only you could draw,
that's the infuriating thing: ickle fish
enmeshed in thick beard,
limbs in seaweed stookies—
in your pocket two jostling crabs.
Shoes salted, teeth gooped,
a beatific smile pious
as a new kite.

Skipper, this is how I imagined
you'd be found, having undergone
an aquatic mummification
you'd overseen personally,
fastidiously; a lewd merman
belching by your flank.

The *big question* was not
whether we wanted to spot you—
like a stricken porpoise or seal
too curious—but whether, if we did,
to throw you back
or take you home for supper;
the colours having shifted.

Yesterday's battering
whittled to a scorch of hours,
snuffed to a wound. No.
More than that—this purse of love,
pilfered by another universe
neglecting to leave a note;
body-break foil-wrapped.

On a balmy Thursday night in May,
after a second day of searching,
abrupt waterworks beneath
a lamppost in Leith, a cauldron
of light wombed around life's
whipping, ripe bawling.
I took the call. I'll admit,
I'm relieved it wasn't me.

Time Travel's Train Travel

Me n' you wir aw'wiz on
that Glasgow to Edinburgh commute—
ranked each locomotive into sitting
spots, bore mark to arse, totem talk
to match. From slow-spoken words, us
dripping dipping into each other's
eyes, to pure blabber, busy
as the chimney pots. The silliest
most serious of patter.

So how wiz it no, no easier
fur you tae say to me: *u'm sinking*?
Morning haar finds it easy
ti banish blue fae sky. Outside
& breezy, ghosts still startle geese
out their earthy camouflage.
I heard your woes, each clunk
within the cogs, the toffee coating
crack; but nowt bold enuf
to tear the whole thing down.
Only it did. Which means I
jist missed it—the minatory mauling
as bone bit back at bone.

You've left us aw
behind: astral specks on pit
-bings, the dug's campestral run,
moi—crashing out the journey's
foggy shell. Seven months long gone.
Missing cat not coming
back. I'm trying tae
remember—no 'Lost Please Call'
poster, no neighbourhood do-gooder
or handsome cash reward

16

will bring you safely home.

I finish gabbing to a passenger,
who, for no real reason,
finger-rips a runway
through the window's breathy patch—
a lover's declaration, abandoned,
grease upon the glass.

The Weak's Guide to Cold Showers

This is not a California-sun-sweetened
shower but a patch of cold
in Scotland—Glasgow in January.
Forty-eight months into the fight
and yet to tame my goose squawk
when the gelid needles strike.

So why run this baltic gauntlet?
Well, I relish the daily terror—
wouldn't trade my pimple-skinned
post-plunge thrum for the softest
soapy bum in all the universe.
The goal is to break morning's
womb-warm circuit: bed cocoon
to scalding soak & cold ever
after. I play my hand, call its bluff
with a prayer of fire amongst frost.
Whilst outfoxing the aquatic gladiator
remains chimera, there are tricks
& tools—cerebral apparatus,
transcendental mind-play.

Foremost is music—the right song,
like a spell, has swagger. Make
an entrance, meld the rhythm
with an avatar. On Monday
I am WWF's The Undertaker,
belt snug on muscled shoulder,
led to the ring by a caterwauling
Paul Bearer—a soundtrack of faith
in the win. Tuesday is a stag leaping
into the forest's force field,
eluding eyes & arrows to harp
strings & bell chime. Wednesday

a quest, mythic & oracular,
with a steampunk orchestral score.

Come Saturday lather me in science,
the promise of brain energy,
propagating brown fat—the good
stuff—a hymn of clever old willpower,
circulative stimuli & blood vessel
buffing, the body becoming
as stress-resistant as a rubber duck.

Each week foments all manner
of title shots, rap battles & gangplanks.
Each day into the shower's surf
where within a heartbeat
the torso tautens like pulled rope—
sayonara hot mozzarella cock.
Five deep breaths & the jaw
unclenches, bones
befitting their domino numbers
as skin settles
under something like rain.

So it's done. Alight
in a display of gallantry, wet
champion of particles, having beat
the black dog sans cruelty—
just a lashing of endorphins.

Of the darkest mornings,
when neither science nor
fantasy is impetus enough,
I lunge for fear's panacea,
pull the cord on courage
at all cost. My friend,
who left this world by water by

night like a meteor thrust
into fierceness. Please, can I ask
—did you look to the stars
on the downward volley? I think
you hit the water burning
like lava into ocean: salt
to vapour & off, deadly
in your spectacle.

It's not a superpower what can be
conjured from a mottled mix
of love, pain & desperation,
but I'll tell you one thing, whether
meek, bawling or blooded,
thanks to you, no cold shower
has bested me yet.

storm above johannesburg

naissance
> what starts smaller than a slug in its ninth symphony
> becomes too big to be drawn in anything but fat crayon.
> the biggest storm in forever bedevils boots then
> an entire city. comes from nothing, same way ego comes
> from nothing—furtively, dreaming in gold.

>> *jonathan slams the '84 benz to an*
>> *emergency stop. our bodies thrust*
>> *forwards, his tots yelp. the old windscreen*
>> *wipers bungled, full obfuscation—we're*
>> *bathroom-door blind.*

stage one
> keening sky rasps. tents collapse into wraith shapes.
> the tempest turns the air gun-hungry. bang.
> a coke can increases its violence. bang.
> the deluge descends flailing—thunderclap, hail
> —a rampage of lightsabres & electric wire.

>> *heads jutting out windows, we captain the*
>> *vessel back to our hotel just minutes from*
>> *this.*

stage two
> glissando, crescendo, old ink gushing out, dynamite
> on a bonfire of voices. kaboom. a fox scavenger
> hauled into the squall, its meat devoured—guts &
> brush spat onto a billboard. some call that art.

>> *flash fast jonathan & his brood cuddled-up*
>> *watching tele in their newly acquired*
>> *room. you & I on adjoining balconies*

donning leopard print robes. ten floors up
in audience with zeus.

ninth

cars alarmed blast banshee, the whale's song bulleted
—prayers smoored by night's vile sauce. infinite
wagner blitzed onto the fifty-four-storey ponte city
skyscraper. the brutalist cylinder bows like a beggar.

we erupt into lavish giggle, can-clinking
hysteria, releasing trapped lightening.
despite the danger, the daggers, we couldn't
have slept sounder.

outro

muck unfixed of its dirt settles. earth negative
versus sky positive shrunk to the maudlin howl
of an animal starved, rain once needle-nasty
now just wool-scratchy on soft pelts.

delight-bright at the breakfast buffet, we
discuss the storm as if it's already buried.

aftermath

if only I'd known we'd survive it, I'd have seen us
swoop at its stormy vitellus—soak our skin
to the blue beneath, tumble over pissing everywhere;
not least for the movie rights, for the starlit fix.

if only I'd known you'd not survive the
next, I'd have eased up on the step count,
quit pushing fruit, joined you in bacon.

Squatting in Rubislaw Den

Of course, I *am* invited, but barely: a so-&-so
tagalong. Besides, there's no squatting
with a housekeeper this scrupulous—shoes

are audited, breakfast logged. Outside,
an Aberdeenshire storm has made a mockery
of the gardener's algebra: amputated branches

strewn across topiary; russets & gold rifled
into rutilance; the honeysuckle slain by a gale
since shrunk to little more than whisker wobble

on a dozing seal in the next town down.
The pond is most heavily handled—
water loss & a debris of petals & spiders

filling its belly. Nibbled by the few surviving
fish, these little dead aliens bespangle
the aquatic undergrowth—their sinking vessels

catch morning's still-standing moonlight
through the film. I'm also here
because of a storm, it blew through &

snatched you away. Though I'm thinking
more of spiders now, their abandoned webs
& spindly falsetto voices—not ones

for sulking, they'd tell me every storm's
a pantomime & today even the rocks are bowed
in rapture. So perhaps better this peripatetic

shape-shifting zephyr for a swansong,
than a portrait fixed by a nail. Settling it,
a tiny frog juts up to sing.

Give Us. Spare Us. Gift Us.

Because it's coming sudden
as a flock of sparrows & cold-quaking
despite the way we dress it.

Spare us: the bumfuzzling, mad moiling
sonic boom of fire treacled
in a tumbler; scorpion strikes
upon the chest; ungodly animal
howl as the news hits.

Give us: a fresh blast of 'Ode to Joy', gold-
finches, cool stream to dip in
when, syrup-sticky, the skin's cooked; that
smile, verdurous as a valley raising up
its earthworms; lips globed around
an ice-cream oyster.

Spare us: the one more & it all comes out
catastrophe—sepulchral slobbering
down the ear of a stranger; the ignominy
as deep despair becomes the dull toll
someone's hot to shirk.

Give us: jacuzzi burble, chintzy diamond
teeth; stories so steak-juicy
the pub windows are steaming up;
the excuse to stay on, to miss
the last train/night bus & not regret it
not a smidge.

Spare us: insipid nostalgia, daft denials
as the fairy lights flicker & fail—old wires,
gnawed to thread, spark-spitting until
the tree's up in a blaze; the alarm

25

too bitter to cry for help.

But if you can't, if the timing's out
& the forecast off, let us have what
we came for should have begged for
moments back. Gift us this:
shame-free & clean
as if cookie-cutter cut.

(A poem with hat tipped to Galway Kinnell's 'Wait')

in italy: toasting to you

like winged bells the sound
    of our ice cubes singing
in swank glasses chutes
    into the breeze
& mischief finds its beat
    as this wild wolf dance
turns smoke signal sigil
    & it jangles like truth
even in the stark heat
    of italian summer
sun-frazzled & wet
    -lipped with grief i can feel
the pull of christmas
    but can you blame me here
in heartthrob cascaroni
    keeping canny to *cinghiale*
my cavalry too kind
    to believe the ghastly
punchline too brave
    to fake it all away
drinking until it dusks
    until fireflies soak
the air in gifts of
    darling
        darling
    gold

Me2Me@12

Muster mettle kid, the morrow's the day radge
Darren & a couple o' cads fae Castlebrae
attempt to chorie yer new Rollerblade Boxcars
wi mottled grind plate.

These blades: pleaded into existence
by a double-down on Christmas
& your birthday. Baileyfield Industrial Estate,
after tea time, when summer light

splits to sticks, is an ace place to skate;
audience-free. So guffaw, fall on yer erse
with impunity. Baileyfield Industrial Estate
is a scunner of a spot to be ambushed

by gnarly kids in shiny skates above
yer skating station. When the pack close in,
muckers Kay Lindsay & Jimbo Grant
flee without so much as a warning whistle—

you'd huv mibees done the same, so dinnae cuss
them fur it. On second thoughts, fuck 'em
just a smidge. Penned in, the geometry
of mischief puddled into shadow. But fret ye not

wee feardie puss, sookle in that lip. It aw works oot.
They frogmarch you to the High Street, to
BG Cycles, custard-pie you wi a bamboozling quiz.
The cads paint a crime-riddled scene, in it

an offering; salvation. Whit they'll propose is:
if Frank here bricked the windae, shattered it
to confetti, & Sid there done the owner in—what
would you pillage from the stash? I've not

a cunting clue what you chose, let's say skates:
boot golfball-white wi wheel frame golden—
a price mark three times ower any blag.
Now wait, summon the gut, there will be a

pensive silence, snide glances in an arcane
language—feel it throb in chuckleberries.
And then, at last, bravo young stargazer,
yer hypothetical half-inch is steely sanctioned.

With a caution not to be so reckless, you're set
loose—a jot more jaguar, a sliver less deer.
Ease that stiffened heart, ameliorate, you will need
this pluck in the years tae come.

Not far from here, on Porty Beach, a sperm whale
will wash upon the shore, nicked in the neck &
bled dry. Surrounding the fleshy corpse, a throng
of folk will be issued the lugubrious reminder:

even giants die. Over yonder is the Forth Road Bridge,
here you'll lose another giant to the same sea
whose salts prick glister into the skin.
When it happens, take each hand giein,

seize upon their love—you'll need love—every
slice of sapience you can get those softy mitts on.
And remember how you skated off that day
heid held high, spry, feeling free.

weird things I am jealous of when wee

the sloppy beard of toothpaste foam cousin

Kevin cultivates when brushing his teeth

Hastie's early burst of pubic hair

despite being surreptitiously ridiculed for having

a cock-zone equivalent to a hirsute dad

the fetishization of Wrighty's asthma inhaler at PE

Daniel for perpetually having an empty house

& getting to cook unlimited micro-chip dinners

Wrighty for being crowned second-hardest in the class

whilst being deified for his abhorrence of violence

Laura for believing such mores

as rubbing lavender between the palms before a race

undoubtedly makes you run faster

Dove's esoteric thoughts on fry-ups

Wilson for laughing so hard he pissed himself

during our Zelda gaming marathon

catching my stopped clock of an eye for sanction

& with permission given pissing & laughing

all the harder exhibiting his unabashed hunger

for fun leaving me full of mirth & chuckle

knowing fine well in his place I'd have been shame

-ridden & ducking for cover heavy with my hang-ups

whilst his chipper grace made of him the hero

I wanted to love him for being

Tough Mudder (the jobby poem)

Thirty-minutes wrangling atop the sharp plastic rim
marks me like a burn.

None the wiser, Class Primary 2a rattle in debate
over the lore of *Biff, Chip & Kipper*.

Meanwhile, I'm pushing into my lightless depths,
where haemoglobins hightail

past braced bones until battle-ramming into
a cement-solid matter.

It was really, really stuck, the manky assailant—
constipation unlike any I'd known

all these six long years of sphincter stretched
to a flamed thread. Vulcanised, I could

feel its gigantics own me, refusing to twitch,
the softness of my vessel cowering

around such girth. Out enough to cast a shadow
on the toilet's throat

yet more abundantly still within. A cumbrous bee
thumps against the window printing

a crest of pain. Taunted by wind, crisp packets
skittle against the wire fence

working themselves deeper into its trap. My toes'
mycelial networks trigger an alarm.

I'd been uncommonly long & so Hastie is sent
knocking, dispatching teacher's concern.

How could I tell him I was exorcising the body's
vile mulch—fighting yet failing.

Despite my muteness he heard his fill, the shiver
of fear rankling my jaw tolled the lock.

Lachrymose & radishing, what I needed to say
—in place of nothing—was send forth

the gut's pyroclastic surge, fetch me a soft-edged
spoon; sorry for all of this.

What I required was wizardry, a time-travelling
Tardis—what they retrieved was

my squeamish big sister. Having been born
impertinently into her second birthday,

she'd not forgiven me, wouldn't have had me
made of chocolate & winning races,

never mind blubbering, birthing a blood otter.
If only I could have

chopped the head off it, stuffed its tail back inside.
But no, & so, quite rightly, my sister

bolted—incredulous, revolted, seething—ready
to denounce me with greater gusto

than ever. Feel free to call this what it is: a boss
baddy, sewage-ugly. I'm not sure how long

passed—barricaded in the cubicle—before my mum
came on a rescue mission.

I'm not sure how she unfudged the unfudgeable
—I remember once shitting in a hot bath;

wasn't that. Regardless, the murky business was
shrift handled and she had me believe

I'd shown bottle: calling for help, stottering off
—not hiding the hurt nor frowning either.

we can't plan our hunger nor where it takes us (aged 8)

The temptation to push a little further
& firmer than we ought to
—to stand on a frozen lake
& smash through the ice or plunge
our hands into wet cement—
is what left me imprisoned
in a Sproftacchel: a face-in-the-hole
picture board. My head,
rusted screw-nut, stuck.
The multi-muscled neck, in all
its lissom glory, shackled to a still.

As with every lamb caught in a fence
there are gawkers & mockers,
preachers & heroes—an unending litany
of jailbreak accomplices. First
came a farmer in mittens of butter,
second a gardener with bucket
& soap, in her shadow a cook
in oil-slicked marigolds,
then an off-duty firefighter
arms barrel-broad. No luck,
still stuck. My mum, placating
a bout of bawling, coaxed out
a thrawn smile. Whilst Laurel & Hardy,
due any minute, never showed
—just an oaf of a Dobermann
that licked me to soup as a coterie
of crows cut curses above.

By the time the tool-kitted ranger came
I was neither fighting nor falling.
Unfixed from the offending headpiece

it dawned upon me,
I hadn't the foggiest whose body
held me hostage—matador,
pirate, princess, clown—
nor the picture we cast.

Swedish Fitta

In high school I was called a *Swedish cunt*
by Simon Angelosanto. If I took
umbrage, sought redemption,
Santo would fight me after school
down the Porty Arcade. Vexed
as my Danish ancestors might be,
blootered in Valhalla, there was no brawl.
I did want to be hardy, loved *Rocky*,
the fire in duelling over something cheap,
but the walk was coarse and I'd seen scraps
weaponized & broil to a razor. Besides,
it was my squeeze the French fuck
hankered after—to whom the fight
would have left me plug-uglied.

Funny thing was, after being dumped
during first year uni, it was Simon
summoned me to Glasgow
for a weekend's succour—oiled my springs
on the Union dancefloor, willed in
new pulls. And the next morning
fed me filthy buck-up, a roll called
Monster, a theatre of surfeit: square
sausage, bacon, black pudding, haggis,
egg & burger—the behemoth bap,
double-buttered, heavy as an anchor.
Each baleful bite more macabre
than the last. *That'll see you right*,
he crooned, *no crying,
just keep grinding until it's gone.*

Simon is a dad now, I always
liked him, runs a caff, filled rolls
—blood, fat & muscle—his nostrum.

Eat into the ache, fortify the gut,
sorcery itself. I wonder,
had that always been the plan,
and was I the first to be fed?

Too Close for Jesus

Sitting in a car hugging too close for Jesus to come
between us, Danny unpacked the tête-à-tête
he'd be marinating all day.

Don't lose your accent.
Don't come back sounding like a smug toff cunt.
You're just as good as any of them.

Being seventeen was over, high school
finito, though the building still loomed above us
like a beleaguered lung, waxed black

from a lift explosion—the old scuzzer wore its scars
well. Words imparted, Danny alit from the vehicle
(a Ford Fiesta borrowed from my mum)

smirking & a little stoned. Theatrically, he loped
into a fake trip—gauging my reaction,
chuffed by the cheeser—clattering

through his parents' front door.
What Danny really meant was: remember me
where you're going / don't let this friendship

drown / is it hanging in the balance? He
wasn't far off. University's collegiate societies
staged themselves supremely: monarchs-in-waiting,

vintage port at high table; bean snobs, dress robes
& gags about rowing, in Latin. I was
ensorcelled, he'd seen it coming—the tow,

the pull & shift, the cobbled street's brute bumps,
the whole rumbustious megillah. Nearly

cast myself out, chasing it: a more regal decking.

But Danny, pain in the hoop though he was,
haemorrhoid of hope that he is, resurrected
that book still barking in my bones.

The one where yer man—a sort of Highlands
Spartacus—bellows *I am the Pict* at some fish
in a river, which I didn't fully grasp yet knew

to be big, to be rippling, akin to having skin
in the starlight. Love for the faces
we're not *yet* rushing back to.

parklife

a kid
       squat down on the edge
       of a kerb wonderdrunk
       from slapping a gutter puddle
       with a stick *la-la-la*-ing up
       towards the roof of a tree
       she can't fathom the crown of
the river kelvin
       writing scripture
       performing miracles
a feral cat
       on the windowsill of the park
       warden's cottage scowling in
       at a spoilt pet's sleeping spot
       imagining such easy dreamies
       paw prints mark the glass
the ghosts
       of snowmen
a hippy scavenger
       holding a grimy rock
       up to the light
       shaking off its dirt bunnies
       until shot through with flakes
       of irradiant opal
just a crow
       without its metaphor for grief
fox
       strutting insouciant until changing
       trajectory as if hearing carols
       in the distance & deciding
       to track them
a black bench
       with your name on it
an old can

of irn-bru wibbling
on its bars
come to think of it
it's just like
the gloaming
to make everything appear
more tigery
how quickly we come out
of the moment how long
before it truly lets us leave

The West End's Great Leaf Harvester

Good morning sweet nectarine sun,
is how the trees beckon light rippling
in the grassy Kelvingrove parkland.

Of course, these barked codgers,
such consummate feeders,
are guzzling more than water
& sunlight. The whole forest's veins
fattened by the secrets they snatch out
air's gummy library—stories
sooked in through the leaf's stomata
& backed up on the bough's
prodigious hard drive.

Take that couple of picnickers
—spines to soil, chasing stars—
they spilled everything
that twilight conflab. Hyena jaws
hung hope-open, their gutsy scruples
now part of the magnum opus
of a stubborn birch.

Come autumn, the trees unhoard
their cache of scandal. & me,
I'm here stuffing my satchel
—the West End's Great
Leaf Harvester, a cat for company,
gazing through knotholes,
sampling the arboreal sherbet.
For every shopping list eavesdropped
there's a gobsmacker of a tryst;
for every whimpering soliloquy,
lodged in the sycamore's throat,
there's a twist of miracle toffee.

43

I test the product—plug my ear
into the leafy loot. *Oooh*,
by the fizz of it, brimful.
A robust blow & out its midrib
hymns all the drama my work's lacking.
I'm soon shaking the trunk until
a passel of leaves parachutes down.

The cat, sultan-plump, already
a blackbird in its greedy gut,
begins swiping for the falling amber.
It pins one to soil, punctures
its papery edge & darts off
prize in mouth. As it rubs
its moggy face in the dirt,
I pounce for the treasure—claws
thrashing, fast-fanged. I miss.
Alongside a garnish of grass
it chomps back the leaf I know to be
this story's happy ending—stem
cigar-snug betwixt its lips.

The Innocent Railway Tunnel

Soon as in it, cold grips the bones & dark
clamps the eyes; our skin, goosebump-riddled
on this satsuma-scorcher of a day.

Unadulted, my gang of four are braced on bikes.
The dare is abject, thralling—to cycle through it
in relay formation; the next boy

not leaving until their forerunner reaches the finish
light. The cruellest of us already
knows weakness festers best sequestered.

It was darker then, Scotland's first railway tunnel
—innocent only on account of the horses
it abused: muckle carriages beast-drawn in an age

where steam engines remained invader species.
Staring down the 518-metre-long shaft, bored
through bedrock, exposes the toatyness

of our courage. The bull bars on my Raleigh
Outlander—this year's tenth birthday present—
not fooling anyone, when there's fear enough

to ring the teeth. I wasn't first, that was something,
but second behind the bravest,
that was worse. Powering off, he was wise

to the subterfuge incline, the snide gradient
that would soon be thrashing my marshmallow
calves. Us watching aghast—pusillanimous

to a pin-drop—as our self-appointed leader
completes the challenge in record time.

Him now howling for me to *move it!*

The tunnel—a voice-carrying impresario—
puts his echo in me, like a bullet. Me,
procrastinating, fidgeting into position,

again, then again. After all, this is a tunnel
for a train never coming to a station no longer
there. Overhead, Samson's Ribs—the gigantic

rock formation—like an avalanche caught
in a photograph. Its load coming down upon us
would be the easy way out.

With a quiver of sound my prayer is pitched
into its goblin gutter. I'm pedalling now.
My stomach burls, hunger-haunted,

the chain whirls, faster than ever—
for what is the chill that stiffens our bones
if not a cause to quicken?

The Skittle Boy's Code of Conduct

There is no official skittle boys' code of conduct,
but if there was I'd have been its draftsman.

Chief Ballboy at the Sheep Heid Inn skittle alley,
Duddingston Village, Edinburgh—February '97

through May '01. Mum had to fib to get me in—
thirteen & over, they said, me a fresh twelve with

the mendicant's guile. In skittles, there's no holes
in the ball, that'll catch folk. Some sanctimonious

prick will sucker-shame the newbies for not having
known this, but don't fret, he's pure bombast—

I've seen him gutter punk & spider. Besides,
I'm the authority here, brimful of pointers,

you only need ask. I like to natter, we're not
Megabowl robosetters—there's no such sophistry.

Me & my pal will simply pop out from behind
bulwarks at the business end of this timber catwalk

& get things going again. As your eye's arrows
sharpen to a blade, I'm already down there,

thirty feet away, in another universe, guessing
your numbers. The wee balls are nifty, palm

bombs, blazing like bolides, but they're capricious
too, & the ogres that toss them need

careful watching. With the bigger balls,
it's between the legs or flumed down the wrist

so it sings in the skin. Pinch the fingers to a beak
& hold the pose, go contrapposto if you can.

& don't worry if I'm scudded in the shin, so as not
to cry I'll pretend a bully's watching.

It's a well-rehearsed heroism, though spying this
you could issue a wink. I'm not sure which wood

the alley's born of, but I do know all its arcs
& contours, why it creaks, where it clenches,

its anfractuous plot. If you're kind, I'll use
my mind to steer the ball—a telepathic hijacking

of secret slant & torque. Of the truculent,
the impolite, that bowl through the break,

proclaiming without asking: *ack he doesnae mind,
paying him are we no?!* Let me tell you,

I may be too meek to put a stop to it but
rolling back the ball I'll be aiming for your fingers.

& another thing, it's £10 per ballboy, one boy
per lane. To the chancing cads that book just me

then play at both—working my body
to exhaustion on promise of a tip—you're ill-fated

for *The Book of Cursed Bowlers*. FYI
this pin monkey isn't pining for a click of extra

cutter but a comrade by my flank.
It's my first taste of power & I'm using it cunningly

to fill the pockets of friends & friends
coveted. It's thirsty work, when you're three hours

in the firing line. I may be young but I'll take
that half-shandy. I've quaffed more sweet nectar

than most my age. Even, once, straight beer.
With the gold coin & shrapnel, you might see me

buying cigs out the machine by the disabled loo
—please don't tell anyone. I sell them for 50p

a pop at school. Same rules apply. I love it here,
even *I* don't know how much just yet. I love it

at Christmas when the boots clomp in snow-
sodden & the quickest way to heat the heart is

by chips or hugging. I love it in summer,
when giddy the light falls over itself to get in first.

Under this gabled roof, I get braver, brave enough
to scar the initials of the seraph I will worship

forever into the rear deck, two sets of letters
marking our lore—loose for any charlatan

to broach & broadcast. Only they don't, but there's
a chance & that thrills, stills, & kills me.

Just before my sixteenth birthday I'll shepherd
my last game, departing the profession crassly

for a weekend job at Next, back when Next
was all the rage & the sale crowds needed to be

police-controlled. After all, a bolder brag
than a high street discount simply didn't exist.

Or so I stupidly thought, until the day it dawned
upon me: I s o l d   u p   c h e a p.

da capo

again
    it came   from a tree
        uncurtaining
         espousing
           branch
           leaf
            seed
            sap
changing its clothes
          canon
              dominion

             buoyed by birdsong
        skinny-dipping
into the season's new
light

   naked   just to start
   dressing   again

Freckle at The Centre of The Sun

The Queen's Drive's top lip pouts
above Holyrood Park, bites at a rise
of 252 metres. Edinburgh's gallery seats
—the vagrant fancy of Prince Albert,
once crowned Europe's champion
carriage road. I'm on its philtrum

watching smoke lurch soft spirals
across the crust of Duddy Loch.
Ominous billows rent to gaunt
ghost fingers, the source unknown.
Swift as I shimmy, it'll be vulgar minutes
before the stomach stops needling.

As a pup, I remember this park's epic
fires, scorch that shred miles of gorse
—verdant & buttery—to charred broccoli.
A chum of mine once the culprit:
we fled, took to hiding, remerged
snivelling like victims, tiptoeing
into a dystopic shadowland
of our own creation. Everything dead
& smouldering as if the volcano
had come again.

From today's vantage:
the loch's a smoking cauldron,
the hidden blaze untouchable,
but by boulders I'll try. Heaving
breathless, around the mountain's final
bend, the global volume nearing
mute, in the torturous clutch
of a *hold, hold, hold...*

It's a campfire, controlled,
contained, toaty. Kids shin-high
could leap it, ash that would hardly smear
in sand. Encircling this flamed freckle,
a cabal of birdwatchers
jaunty on hot coffee, no idea how vast
the winnowing smoke splinters,
its sidling of guilt.

We Are Other People to Other People

Fifteen years after first asking
I still wobble on whether my dad
gets lonely at golf, the long weight
of a duffed drive, the lost ball's
penalty point. That dog of his
killed by a car, unmourned
for fear of the slagging.
A reprinted requiem of photos
of Dad in the scratty breeks
umpteen sizes over, belted
by rope. Is dirt-poor & Danish
really a master caveat, a bung so as
we might continue to issue emotion
like a weather forecast?

Our language moving with us—
through & past us. The fickle currency
of rain: not for hiding from
but hiding in; capable
of stream & harvest whilst sticking
to puddle & pot-plant. Dad,
have I ever really asked you?
Don't go before I do,
before I come fish-belly-up
wings clipped & straight to it.
We snorkel before we scuba
because a beginning is a limit—
not a deep dive we'd both get lost in,
just a lungful. Just a gasp.

Placenta & Chips

Christ! We just wrapped it in newspaper & tossed it in the fire
—my gran blurts back boon when I recount, half

-kidding, my attempt to finagle a placenta
to make lasagne from. *Should have seen your grandad's face*

when he was handed it to deal with—placenta,
in a newspaper cocoon, hoisted out the kitchen hatch.

Still thinking in food, this summons for me, not
the image it should have (a flame-winged phoenix

rising from the ashes), but the vision of a paper-bound
fish supper. Rather, the trauma of a supper, barely

touched, yanked off a friend by his rancorous Da
& lobbed into the blaze. He'd been remonstrating,

the friend, all faux bratty on account of a paltry serving
of chippie sauce & lack of pickled onion—theatrics,

intended only to beguile. I nearly wept for him, who,
unbeaten, chose instead to shine; taking artful ownership

of the botched performance. So steeled with pride,
he refused not to watch it burn, refused any bite of mine.

An act I heralded as a keystone for bravery. Now
bringing the conversation back into the room, I intuit

what my grandad had prophesied watching those
blades of flame strip placenta from its parcel

like a butcher's magic trick. Its numinous glow
of heather amongst the whisky-coloured scorch

could have turned ugly under the wrong set of eyes.
But not here, not with hunky George waiting

to be summoned to hold his wee baby. My auntie,
whom he'd meet once she'd been sponge-cleaned &

swaddled in a home-knit. Hearing the chime of his name
would be knowing the occasion's real 'heavy lifting'

had already been handled.

One More Open Gate

Isobel Wylie Hutchison (1889–1982)
pioneer, botanist, painter, poet, voyager

who is blood moon whisperer, lore makar,
Saturn-eyed, owl-eyed, willow-catkin-saxifrage-eyed
—so many monikers, it's humbler not to list them.

Isobel, privileged as you were, it did not spare you
death's savagery, its graceless aching—
father first, then brothers both. Perhaps grief
sent your mind fleeing before the body could:
Edinburgh to John O'Groats, walking
with the spirits—deep north, all ways north,
60° Shetlandic north, Leith to Copenhagen,
hella north; norther still.

Isobel, first Scotswoman to set foot on Greenland,
collecting flowers on the tundra, greeting
cherishable humans and—dressed in
those famous seal-skinned breeks & island knits—
dancing reels imported by Scottish whalers.
Banshee fiddles, the squeeze box,
figures-of-eight and dos-à-dos.
Did their melody dial the heart's hotline
into your bale of memories of home?
More likely, the other way around—back
in Caledonia pining for this
moonlit frozen ballroom.

Isobel, watching the river that carried you
gush ice into the fjord, feasting
on boiled salmon, hand
-torn, bones becoming
toothpick spears. The upturned boat:

57

a windbreaker, its sealskin belly drying
by the fire's fuzzed amber
as oil lamps turn tents to lanterns.
But it's the welkin, of course, that wins
the night—Aurora above like a giant ship
of light, land the bottom of the ocean:
electric seaweed ribbons of emerald
& amethyst. Dragon's breath.
The silence explodes with Greenlanders
baying up at stardust glaciers.

The Northern Lights are Merry Men,
they tell you, souls of the dead
playing games with the head of a walrus.
What a night's kip
that must have been. How many ghost ships
sailed by you sleeping? How many dark shapes
sucked into the deep?

Isobel, traveling by dog sled
by the rope of arctic wind, towards each
long unopened gate, inking letters home,
scrawls to end: *that's if I ever make it back.*

I wonder what you'd reckon to us, so
starkly elsewhere, eyes sunk into a screen,
uploading the lens's latest
capture. It's not all bad, I'd tell you, sometimes
we too are watching dolphins leap, ships
overcome pelagic trials, posting pictures
that might combat the long loneliness,
but not before we chrome-filter those fuckers,
revving up the faint glow
of the *cruising stars* to a red-gold
sweet-shop-bright.

Isobel, it just takes some getting used to.
Did I mention, we found water on the moon?

The Last Post

Isobel Wylie Hutchison (1889–1982)
pioneer, botanist, painter, poet, voyager

It's in the Arctic we find you,
on a boat called *Trader*, flanked
by myth—the ghost ship, *Baychimo*,
abandoned years back; caught
in a whorl, engulfed by the freeze.
The crew had no other out
but to flee the floating village
carrying only their bones for survival.
They made it, battled blizzard to shore,
but the ship vanished; a giant free
from its chains, in its wake
the busted apparatus—a mountain
of cracked ice, a hundred
(could have been a thousand) feet high.

Henceforth, *Baychimo* is glimpsed
spectrally, in disbelief, dusted by moon,
tied to its magnets, clacking
like a bell, its phantom
contours at last visible.

Beneath a birdless sky, Isobel, you
ascend its rickety ladder, boot crunching
deck frost, conjuring Captain Hook,
Robert Louis Stevenson. Where voices
roistered, not a single orphan echo
nor a Christmas cobalt
blue, just the humourless chill.

Already, Inuits have scoured
Baychimo's gallimaufry, left things

unworthy of their weight: caribou
skins, mineral ore, sinew thread.
A haul formally known as beautiful
greased garish by the lonely in it, the unwant
and portent of flowers on a bridge.
Eerier still, the table dressed with silver
laid for breakfast, a harbinger
for what the stomach can do
without—hope, like eggs, cools cruelly.

As if plucked from some oceanic film noir,
a typewriter, then another,
rusted fangs still sharp enough
to bite upon the paper, crunch
letters into curlicues, words shattered
to shards in a dream
long gone—for a litter unlogged
the machine's tongue-droops.

Isobel, fits you like a crown, this gallantry.
Whereas Pete and Karri purloin
the captain's compass, you harvest
'Hudson Bay'-headed paper,
turn the blankness with a *Dear Hilda*
dispatch, a sisterly spin on this
most exciting & uncommon adventure.

Isobel, a crotchet: perhaps
it would have been mercy
to have torched the ship? Ended
its bruising vigil: infinite
pounding off the ice
in a skin of old scars. Yes,
I'd have razed it to ashes, yes,
sent it yowling like a starved cat,
past krakens, into darkness

so deep and viscous
it's yet to be imagined.

You knew better,
saw the lost dog in it,
the magic torque, hidden heartbeat
of its icy hoop ringing
like Saturn's bent halo—that singing,
clever fox, you heard music.

(The Baychimo trade ship was evacuated in 1931. Isobel
boarded in 1933. It sailed uncaptained until 1969.)

The Secret Life of Balconies

Little boxes full of stars. They're up there,
spaceship fleets of them: concrete sages;
mobster floats; hoverboard tapestries
of the twilight. Each a sliver of sovereignty
scrappled back from the ether—a deckchair,
fairy lights & a smoking bucket.
The best ones are scanty, towel-sized
& jam-packed with chintz, blasted by sunlight's
lavender. The very best are pullulating
with plant life, pollen thronging nirvanas
for our insect saviours.

Little carnivals of the imagination. I love
spotting them, sneaky & incongruous,
catching the eye of their mystic jockeys
—hauling us together: *I see you, moon rider*,
in that string vest, oily chest, those magic
tan lines, tinnie in hand. Love it when they
thunder back: *I see you, day drifter*—a magisterial
wave as if signalling for the games to begin.
The can, rinsed of its elixir, raised up,
up, higher than the sun dares set,
inches from a jealous god.

Galway Gull

A great gull, wings outstretched & cruising chipper,
prangs into a car on the Salthill Road. I'm out
my hangover in an instant

wincing at the collision's bruit. The crack (bird
belly on car bonnet) like wood splitting
in the throes of a fire.

The car not stopping as tendons begin
to audit bone-break. Almost angelic,
our pudgy bird settles on the tarmac

like a nesting mammy—furls its wings, blimps
its chest, those daft yellow waders hidden
from sight. By all appearances content

as a baked tattie slathered in butter & cheese.
The shock of morning's sea swim is back
bugling my lungs, as two cars come

careering round the bend. Both vehicles shudder
to a halt for the beast unbudging—knowing
nothing of its bloodspill its smooshed

raspberries inside & no hollow left not wet
with pain. The drivers toot, slalom past
& onwards. Cozening the crowd,

the button-beaked creature looks more like
it's welcoming new life than losing a shot
at old. Or perhaps I just mistook its

queer countenance—a drifting into the ghost
of itself—being so desperate to see such

peacefulness at the end.

Good Days & Bad

the bad days

        are samurais
           lurking in shadow
        pavement sink
           -holes broken-down
        busses & bath bomb elegies
           kerplunk no amount
        of mirrors make the big
           cage big enough

    the good days

                play like a flute
                    the gooey nonsense
              of kissing silly tongue
                    -sprung gravy of life
              thickening unapologetically
                  doused over fluffed
              potato bodies as sun's
                    lightening riverdances
              on people's faces

    the bad days

        wash off like sand
           in the shower orbit
        total then not at all
           skin-slashing poltergeist
        hex hefting stowaways
           gnawing from beyond
        in paean to the
           gnarled nasty cold

    oh but the good days

                    blunt any scour

66

trump the itchy grain
with toasted beach plus ice-
cream sea plunge
& a bone-brightening
towelling clever as
silver spider wire as
tea leaves slapping
water with a cadence

amazing
how day   turns when
your head   heavy &
purring   naps
on my lap   & like a mug
prints me   with its hot
circle your hum flourished
flesh moved to a whisper
I whisper back
make this the heat
I am found
in

red lipstick

red lipstick caked across the mouth
of an entry wound implies vileness implies
shots fired but in some cases is just jam
frothed with sugar—syringe-pumped

into the pastry's capacious gut. red lipstick
on a pout pleading is only surplus atoms
to the words that follow—gloop trailed
over teethy cliffs. red lipstick

on the o-shaped pucker of a lifebelt
draped above the clyde—the number
on the samaritans' sticker vandalised
by someone with a viper in the throat

callous from too long untouched. red
lipstick on a solo padlock initialled
& kissed for luck—not on paris's *pont
des arts* but cuffed to the grillwork

of glasgow's bell's bridge. no galaxy of keys
dropped into the water causing rancour
to the po-faced pike. no metallic remora's
plus-tonnage wrestling the structure

into the sludge. no sinking at all just
red lipstick framing a promise
likely already broken yet to hungry eyes
still piping hot as if fresh-baked.

The Elder Wand

it's
the way we
parse the drop beyond
the ledge then imagine falling
eyebawling horizon's furthest fleck only to
walk away drunk with life the pining syllables of
the last stanza struggling to consolidate to cauterise
and box up everything unspoken it's the
feeling of both rapture and desire in
reading a better description than
your own best description
of a fallen
star

it's
the way we
parse the drop
imagine falling the
pining syllables struggling
to consolidate everything
unspoken the feeling
in reading a better
description of
a fallen
star

the way
we drop syllables
unspoken description
better a fallen
star

a
drop
u spoke
be a
st
a
r

after the fall

the bruise of you seeps beneath my body's bonnet, hot
-wires its sinews, commandeers the bones. up
top, a hubcap of blood blackens into

a dark uniform. sneakily moonish, the bruise speaks
through every flex, because who doesn't push
down when the pressure's rising.

but a bruise is just a button, a public face, & the
throb of you is not without its alms.
the way the whole mess mends

by mottling: from rain-soaked slate to a gentle-mulberry
-almost-fuchsia, ripple of copper, rake of rusty
dawn. mere days into the corporeal fracas

my skin, the little traitor, near swallows the evidence.
though the bump still bellows below deck: a gurgle,
a swansong hissing in the follicles,

that little glow-in-the-dark star: limp & lifeless until its
ultraviolets are fully charged. That said, the bruise
of you is so very welcome to squat

in me, its twang through flesh a shot of something
sorely missed——a heavy-footed hare
chasing the smudge of dusk.

Scotland's Premier Ocean Vuong tribute act is walking to the ring

A few steps into the stuttering light
—the speakers blaring Ocean Vuong's poem
'Ode to Masturbation'—I begin my levitation.
Suited in my tear-proof birthday boy best,
my underdog's cape raining down
a sequined joy. Reaching ringside, I shatter
the crowd's rasp barrier, bounce down
upon the ropes, purring jubilant as a box-fresh
electric bike. Bamboozling my opponent:
bleating like a lamb preening its coat
for rescue—in the hope they might stop
gunning for my youth, release
some enmity & join me.

My perfect plié catches the gimlet eye
of the chubby-cheeked clock. I glance
a palm across my opponent's chest
so as the sonorous hands of time know
where to enter. The bell's trill sugar-pumps
the blood yet even the hurt hungriest
in the crowd are now twinkling twice before
hooting for anything beyond a deft exhibition
of antler clash; the percussion of bodies soil-soft
turned hoof-hard. & just as the poem ends with
a word nailed to its meaning & lives, so too does
our verdict, propelling past mere numbers
to where scores become notes of a song.

here in a glasgow tenement—not asleep, not awake either—

hear

sheet creases tattoo aphorisms on my sweet birthday suit

hear

snowfall on the rooftop this tenement doesn't have—a crown coeval with the floor of a neighbour who hasn't danced in days

hear

a black beetle with butterscotch eyes assert its dominance over the weakling woodlouse

hear

the silvering screech of my eyebrow hair rake over umpteen deserted follicles—a.k.a. graves

hear

someone ask *are you busy?* when i'm very busy, and me intending to answer *busy as migrating geese as trap-dodging bears as desperate bellies*, but instead muttering *a bit busy but not too busy*

hear

my spirit animal settle on a bullfrog: an invader species known to barely slumber—unwittingly violent, green upper lip

hear

the shriek of scalpel as my enemy cuts, rubbery, the guts from my bullfrog; not to eat, simply to chew and spit back out

hear

the sun flare, knowing if it wasn't already on fire we'd burn it

hear

a threshold gatekeeper—warden of the unkempt feelings between dreams & dying—clock off with a raspy laugh

hear

your voice remind me not to worry because we can nap—
napping helped make us, is best done nudey: my hot balls
against your back

hear

my spangled heart: thistle, warble, then mend with the
memory, like weary knees pressed into familiar dirt, below
an altar, or a tree

psalm on descent

i vow

to never pooh-pooh the runways of cloud ribboned over the places we're racing past—never is their scrim too thin; never are they unfit for sledging

to always be parsing the hinterlands for pagan orgies & the shock blue of pool parties

to never fly without flakes of sand nuisancing my socks, tumbling out turn-ups, in reminder to get back to the beach

to always be the one *really* steering this bird—the gut's joystick, unlikely captain

to never attune with the thunder, which is often not thunder but propellor garble partaking in a great operatic gloat

to always be ready to talk down the cursed swan or kamikaze kite looking to dance with death

to never make an ally of the restlessness in the news we're couriering—fleshy messengers above the rain

to always be kneading some mangled truth into a shape that fits the conscience forty thousand feet above the consequence

to never take for granted a safe landing: the vessel, steeled, crashing to tarmac determined to perdure

to always be listing the people i've not yet loved enough; descending together; in my body, a prayer: *may the absences i cast be balanced by the voids i fill*

dear lover

if i die before you, & you can be arsed, please publish
my unpublished poems

because in them is a slew of things said better than the
things i really said

because i'll never read the bad review by 'the forensic
wit' that dresses them down then anoints *him*self for
having the gall to do so

because ted did this for sylvia (& i'm zealot & a sop)

because if i go how i think i go then it's vital that's not
my final floozy word

because there might be enough cutter in it to pay for
costa rica; or, at the very least, a knees-up in a local
tiki bar

because some people will like my stuff because they
liked me even if they don't really like my stuff

because even though the stranger's glance that landed
with a *you're a bit of alright* reverted to a bone-dry *on
closer inspection mibee not* we both still managed a laugh

because at least three of my favourite writers
published their worst work posthumously & i
canonised them for doing so

because a certain someone once thought this blushing
dafty galloping in lithe as a bee-stung donkey was
scrummy

because why the fuck not

because there's a link between how we lament the lost
& the way oysters sex-shift that proves the fecklessness
in buckling your grieving body, & that might yet make
all the difference

because it'll shut the traps of the squiggle of toads
already croaking, *what's all the fuss about, he barely even
published?*

because i am that vain

because there's a poem amongst the rabble that rabbits
on about legacy before letting you know how much i
loved you, when i'll be so dead sorry i cannot

not so much written as gifted

the smell of burnt halloumi in my hair
& seed-speckled shoelaces

vaulting towards my lover
for a voyage down the riverbank

i'm riding this bike like a corsair
of the cycle paths hopping

potholes & snatching blackberries
straight from the bush

in moments like these this work
seems god-given

having used their egg-teeth to tear
through the shell the poems

arrive total & chirruping
caked in chutzpah ensorcelled

i peddle faster & yell into the sun
release these words from in me

Birds & Blowies

Coming—palm cradling
your skull, fingers fed into
the hair's soft grapple—I wind
up the eyes' shutters to see two
fluttering birds, mid-flight salsa,
  meld together like the head
of a tulip; by the time my vision
steadyohs they've either vanished
up a tear duct on the abutting
cottage's thatched roof or, gambol
over, they've returned to their nest
in the chest from which they came.

of Fuck Up

       mistake

born

       of wonder and giddy

shorn

       to spark-spitting wires

blood

       bucket bomb above the soloist brought

down

       on hunched bones by song's echo

turbid

       as the occult world of dark

drinks

       regret's wretched chutney the

bloodied

       crawl from its wreckage the

want

       for quiet wisdom stubborn as cold turf

is

       slit destoned soil can return to its softness

careful

       pain is not trenchant when risking too much

careful

       does not mean no

courage

       is careful love moonquake ripples on

loch

       impressions on skin

hook

       hole fang pit admissions of simmer

dim

       I'm aching careful to tell you *kiss*

kiss

       this

of my own first word

i've not a scoobie
nor does it grate
but i do have suggestions
for the last of them
experiments
in furnishing breath
before the dip of death
mind both still & racing
the way a winter stream
can be frozen on its crest
whilst galloping away
below the ice
    what's more
        when it fades
i've already decided
    my hand will not need held
    my hands will hold each other
who'll be holding my hand

lovers holding hands

these blind instruments
chanced together
acolytes
of each other
held
in the keen
clutch
of a harvest bow
where fingers
stridulate
playing
the flourish
& skin's voltage
scintillates
a spark
for each touch

perhaps behind that mist is a mountain

<u>The journey begins how you'd expect:</u>

later than intended (19:05). Racing time takes us
off-road—us is me, merry, jinking, stocking some
regret—straight up Queen's Drive's vertiginous sling
and into the dead pull of winter: the park at night.

This park, Holyrood Park, a gallus 650 acres: volcanic
rises, eccentric geometry. Under night-time's hex it's
blackout-bolshie, treacherous as ocean.

Lucky I'm armed: mittened & scarfed with hands
hoisted forwards, navigating the thick thick thickening
still. The city can't catch me, it's miles off in spark
& pebble-dash; a thousand tiny embers of Christmas
trees, lighters, lampshades & tellies.

Gums zapped, I take a hard drag on the frost veined
air—inside hot lungs it crinkles then thaws, until old
instinct posts the breathy package back out with a
phosphorescent glaze.

<u>Walking in the sheer dark (no lamp posts no cat's eyes):</u>

i
keep
dropping my eyes to the kerb
spearing the concrete
wrangling for a fix
keep
casting my gaze far as it'll glide
before blinded by black
& boomeranging back

82

                        moon
ever oddly, dithering,   makes an apex
from behind a behemoth lump of molten rock
the hill's creaturions whisk up a virile music and so
killer lens is on them and, by happenchance, on us
who skittle over its grubby gradients

                    moon's a pickled
                    mushroom
                    on squid ink,
                rock salt w-r-e-a-t-h-e-d
            never running out of ways to spill
                    its sauce

            moon's an old goat wearing a young
            kid's face, a mad pet lost in the attic

Spotlights on:

a walker passing // with a hand torch // with a head torch
    // with a mobile phone lightsabre // I'm stubborn stuck
    to keep mine off // and in the camouflage be the plucky
    troubadour // you'd surmise lambasts yappy robotics //
    randy stallion // contactable only when ready to consort
    // one of the coven walking sans illumination // in the
    mottled leather and ebony // eyes desperate & daggering

each heavy tread is a klaxon: skin incoming
bodies passing with last-minute shifts of the shoulder—
mercury—a protean sidestep

each vague shape is an iceberg warning
appearing as if gatecrashing out another realm
making a mockery of dark's infinity
                        and then

gone
disappearing with a
low-toned

    sorry——sorry
scuffle——shuffle

spoken too late & spectral to offer
    any defining glimpse of brain
    or brawn

curious but this is how to walk at
night
    tethered to hunger
    travelling without papers

<u>A reminiscent sort of saunter:</u>

I had hiked this same path in the baby-bunny morning of
the day (08:45) and so revisit a mirage of images captured
of the walkway. Having strode the opposite direction, I flip
the picture, erase my steps as I trace back over them. It's not
reversing time but the other side of everything that led me
here.

Morning feet were weighted, heaved, as if a sleeping cat sat
on them. But night brings a spryness—a spring shovel in each
beating thigh.

'sake, my little hummingbird heart aw flutter & flash
you've served me well today.

Something bizarre happened in daybreak's misty stew. It
was an encounter, aye, that's the best way into it—simple,
then not so simple; ingredients of me & someone unfamiliar

who felt anything but. Who was déjà vu's flashback reverie, congruent marrow, electrons pulled from the same dark sac.

<u>The a.m. encounter. Let me take you back:</u>

When we met, the morning cold was bold enough to graze cheeks & pepper lips. The tree branches creaked like bones needing oiling——their big wooden arms bearing the burden of frost & dew, almost louche with their heavy wet.

And so our paths collided, them staring out into the abyss at the highest point of the walk, nostrils full to bursting.

They stood there like a Griffin after a long flight, bestial yet calm.

I stopped to do my own copycat gawking.
What else would you have me do?

Mist at the edge of the railing hid just how far the fall would be. We agreed on bottomless. Fog swaddled up against us, charting each other's marks like caddish stars hoping to coruscate beyond the constellation. The gaps in them same like the gaps in me, we rummaged around in each other for spare parts.

They smirked, a screwball grin, our thoughts in tune, thinking there could be a residential skyscraper behind that haar; or the headquarters of a multinational corporation; but

being up this high, marooned by acres of parkland, it's more
likely a mountain.

And so it was. We climbed it together. I'll never forget it.
I think this poem is called: perhaps behind that mist is a
mountain.

On the descent, we took a moment to wire deeper in,
stunned by the timbre of the haar; which was mimicking
blindness, masking anything further than an arm's length off.

Loping down this corridor of obscurity was to crash-land into
every moment.

We're stilled by the mellifluous boogie of it

I said

the same still's in being caught off guard
by a banging tune you once smooched clean through—
out the other end with all the possibilities of a river
that meets the sea.

There's no one but us, birds & gorse.

Don't forget what's underneath
they said

moles catapulting earthworms, scraping
through their earthy marathons
at the pace dreams are dreamt when in them.

And dare I say
think of all wonder lost to the quickening pace
of the seconds between waking, accessing the light,
and kicking on the kettle.

What tragedy.

Tragedy

And when the wind blushes up, cuts us out of here,
I'll answer that something you've been waiting to
ask.

A Nordic intruder:

I did my thinking. And that was true for me, true relief.
I pedalo-ed in the ruminative bog of it until my bumper
thumped upon the metaphorical bank, and a new conversation
(the big one) cheeped inside. Cheeped, though it shouldn't.

As fate would have it, misfortune struck before my tongue
wrestled into action. A cocky Swede appeared, ripping through
the cloud curtain.

The Swede had the newest-model camera noosed around his
neck, a Pomeranian in a papoose looped around his chest.
Lanky limbs, multi-pocketed shorts, walking-boot-sandal
hybrids with studded snakes that laced around the ankle; a
bead on his stringy beard.

Him hiking uphill, us trucking down, he stopped, we stopped,
and then the camera flashed off in our faces. In my ire,
I never caught if a finger or a paw pulled the trigger.

This pictorial enternalisation shamed us out our intimacy,
popped the oneiric scene like a yolk on the spear-end of
toasted soldier.

Playing the advantage of the upset, the Swede
fled braggart with his trophy pic.

You better email that to me, I yelled rankled in his wake—giggly
but with barb.

To my surprise he did as soon as the fog swallowed him. The
subject line read: really weird *ja / tack så mycket* for nothing;
which in Swedish means: really weird aye / thanks for
nothing you candy ponies.

After the yelling had flooded out me, I turned to address my
fellow traveller, but they were gone and the quailed grass was
finding shape again.

Of the traveller's absence: I was pining hard.

They left me in an ice-cream flurry tasked with trying to
place the unplaceable.

The rest of the way down, I stomped as if I had stones
in my pockets—ran my memories through a slipstream
a soda-stream a sieve. But the queries pending kept pending.

Back in the now-bow of night (19:45):

>   That's why I'm late and walking this way—starved,
>   wolf-stalking. Why, in certain dark, I'm mapping out
>   their beautiful body. This park's Pygmalion, I envision
>   them like a steeple: cross strong from the people they
>   loved.
>
>   Around this bend my journey's end.
>   A last blast of lunar light comes down

like a saucer of milk c

                    a

                    s

                    c

                    a

                    ding over the rim—

the whole stunning firmament like a great celestial
milk float

its bottles chinking sparkle-crusted glow & slosh into
the interstellar

infinite space vitamins glugged into my bones, suppling
their creak,

wolf-wound licked clean—does wonders the moon

just by landing drunk on the skin.

Fingers locked in mittens, charging up my spells,
I exit the park through the Willowbrae gate
believing in ghosts
more like a seven out of ten
than a five out of ten;
perhaps
ready to remember,
perhaps
not

Mike's Tackle Shop: The Ultimate Reincarnation

On my first trip fishing a williwaw
scuffed the water to a skin
and the loch warden carolled to me
& Ian the Janny: *father & son permit
is it? och aye you can see it in the eyes
such a questing blue.*

Twenty-five years later, in honour of
my birthday, Malachy sculpts a fly:
red wool, gold wire, deer hair,
peacock feather—munificent
as any true friend's portraiture
it's surplus gorgeous.

Mike's laddie Mark became a cage
-fighter, a crevice-gouger
& fish-hooker, bled
his dark liquor onto cheap plastic mats
—but what prosody, what gall.

Fuss-free, many—beautiful—boys
never left the Tackle Shop's
liminal parade, grew wild & schtum,
river too soon. Departed
by king salmon leap, stuffed
to the gills, couriering fear
the way stream smuggles
moonlight—hushing its glow.

Mike's Tackle Shop has closed
down. I've wriggled free
from the slipknot formulae. Unfankled
not unmade. On its very spot
on the High Street now sits

Portobello Bookshop,
where mallets hung
poetry stacks the shelves.

Edinburgh's Fallen

Cockenzie Power Station's twin chimneys
once stood a hundred & fifty metres
above the Prestonpans ice cream van;
a coal-fired colossus billowing clots
of pewter cloud. Profane in its
massiveness, Portobello High School
marred the skyline; no plutocrat,
it earned every inch of its staunch
shadow. Porty's first partisan.

From undefeatable gladiators flaunting
weaponry to clapped-out greyhounds
hiding a limp. When they blew up
the power station thousands revelled,
climbed hills, took to beaches & boarded boats
with picnics; countdowns swelled, misfired
looped back—the beans kept jumping until
BOOM. First fire-dust rifled its gut
like popping candy fed to the swans,
then the chimneys crumbled inwards,
embraced like drunk friends falling
laughing. We surveyed from a verdant
summit, toasted it as Hogmanay,
snogged, watched again on YouTube
with a soundscape in slow motion—
spectral voices mooing as the bricks
unzipped, disappearing behind a powder.
The last opal of smoke the dragon issued
saw it choke on its own ash.

The high school met a more shameful demise,
stripped down in stages over an aeon:
robbed of its cape, finger-bones broken.
Gouged by metal claws until lower

than a double-decker bus,
loose wires fraying in wind ugly
as unfair grief. All the dignity of a tiger
in a cage at a cocktail party;
a crab launched at a rock.

What happened to *Merry Christmas*
tattooed on its brow by some brave
bastard held out a window by their ankles?
What happened to the bats guarding
the greenhouse, the spider plants
that kept growing though creosote black,
fed only fag ends. To the carrier bags
caught on pigeon wire like geese
wrung by the neck. To the slip
in middle of the stairwell, a spit &
piss-speckled portal down which objects
& fluids, like asteroids, flew. Over a thousand
desks extincted, all those names scraped
into their pelts—manifestos, declarations.
What happened to the cupboard
the history teacher shagged a student in,
which definitely happened, Junior assured me,
his sister seen it. Junior with the lisp,
who OD'd. What happened to Junior
besides his dying? To my first kiss,
first punch, first balk at the ache
of the bullied, yen for the far-off,
because we can't plan our hunger
just where it takes us.

Cockenzie was handed a queen's sword
to fall on. Portobello died a death of
a thousand cuts. I'm not saying
I'd switch them, who am I to condemn
the heart of a heretic, it's enough

to be here when they're not.

Acknowledgements

A few of these poems have appeared in such sensational magazines as: *The Rialto*, *The Dark Horse*, *The Poetry Review* and *Ambit*. The paeans to the great explorer Isobel Wylie Hutchison are the result of a juicy commission from the National Library of Scotland. Another poem was galvanised by Cúirt International Festival of Literature. Some of these poems were written on residency at The Curfew Tower (Cushendall) – hat tipped to Bill Drummond for my stint there.

Thanks

Firstly, to my editor and cherished champion, Sarah Castleton – for her spirit, sapience, panache and tenderness in helping sculpt these poems into their most worthy incarnations. I wept a little at your offer letter and everything that followed has been a thrill. Alongside Sarah, my gratitude to all the ace humans at Little Brown/Corsair.

Jon Gray, who has furnished this book with his artistry and illustrations, and who buoys me up with his friendship.

Becky Thomas, my agent, for her aplomb, tenacity and support in helping my weird words find ideal homes.

Hollie McNish, who empowers me in both love and in writing. It's the pleasure of my life this gloriousness you proffer.

Scott, dear H-Craft, I'll never be done missing your chortling pus. My friend, I love you – thank you, thank you, thank you.

Muckle cheers to my poetry group for their many zesty insights – Marjorie, Iain, Francis, Esa; & to Gerry who's kept a look-in since the start.

To all the cats I've taken inspiration from: Merry, Christmas, Fatty Lumpkin, Hally, Bop, & Charlie – even Silvio (the pure diva).